VISIONS

THE
ART
OF THE
QUILT

Deborah Bird Timby, Editor

QUILT SAN DIEGO

◆

C & T Publishing

Belated and double thanks to Marilyn Sidler, my long-time quilting friend and editing mentor, for burning the midnight oil with me for two Visions books.
–Deborah Timby

Editing by Deborah Bird Timby, San Diego, California

Copyediting by Harold Nadel, San Francisco, California

Design-Production Coordination by Jill Maxwell Berry, Artista Artworks, San Diego, California

Photography by Carina Woolrich, San Diego, California
unless otherwise noted

Cover Photo by Sharon Risedorf, San Francisco, California

Cover Quilt: *Firestorm* by Mary Mashuta

Printed in Hong Kong

Published by C&T Publishing, P.O. Box 1456, Lafayette, California, 94549

Library of Congress Catalog Card No. 92-53799
Visions : the art of the quilt : seventy-nine quilts from the exhibition, Visions—the art of the quilt / Deborah Bird Timby, editor ; Quilt San Diego.
    p.   cm.
    ISBN 0-914881-54-X : $19.95
    1. Quilts—History—20th century—Exhibitions.   I. Timby, Deborah Bird.   II. Quilt San Diego (Organization)
NK9110.V53 1992
746.39'049'074794985—dc20   92-53799
                                                                          CIP

ACKNOWLEDGMENTS

◆

Quilt San Diego has been blessed with two things: a powerful vision of how art, especially quilts, enriches our world, and the right people at the right time coming forward to expand that vision into reality. The manifestation of our vision in 1992, Visions–The Art of the Quilt, was made possible by the leadership of a number of individuals and organizations who skillfully ventured into new territory and succeeded beyond all expectations. Among these talented and dedicated people, Quilt San Diego wishes to acknowledge specifically:

- Lynn Johnson, Executive Director of Quilt San Diego and Past President of the Board of Directors
- Deborah Timby, Book Editor and Assistant to the Executive Director
- Members of Quilt San Diego's Board of Directors: Alice Busse, Karen Emberton, Barbara Hartung, Cynthia Hansen, Judy Hopkins, Pat Marean, Patricia Smith, Shirlee Smith, and Julia Zgliniec
- Visions Committee Chairpersons and assistants: Martha Brown, Chris Chase, Lee Ann Decker, Marilyn Henderson, Merilyne Hickman, Dotty Hill, Carole Leffler, Harriet Love, Carol McKie Manning, Barbara McDowell, Susan Plack, Michiko and John Rice, Harriette Schapiro, Diane Stone, and Peggy Walther
- Our generous members, corporate sponsors, and volunteers
- The San Diego Historical Society and Lucinda Eddy
- C & T Publishing.

Finally, Quilt San Diego wishes to recognize the contributions of the hundreds of quilters from around the world who entered their works for display in Visions. Individually and collectively, these quilters create and sustain the vision for "the quilt as art."

Diane M. Seaberg
President, Board of Directors
Quilt San Diego

4

Detail of
REFRACTION #1, #2, #3

CARYL BRYER FALLERT

SAN DIEGO HISTORICAL SOCIETY
PERSPECTIVE

◆

The San Diego Historical Society proudly welcomes Quilt San Diego's third juried exhibition. Our association with Quilt San Diego began several years ago with plans for Visions–A New Decade, an exhibition we were privileged to host in 1990. Today the San Diego Historical Society is again honored to be the selected site for Visions–The Art of the Quilt.

As a local and regional historical society, our mission is best fulfilled when we are able to show how the lessons of the past can be relevant to our modern lives today. Over the past two decades, historians have increasingly moved away from an interpretation of history that merely recounts the lives of famous individuals, epic wars, and political conflict. Now scholarly research has begun to reveal the everyday lives of men, women, and children, providing a means to gain insight into our nation's social history and a better understanding of how all the peoples within our diverse communities share a common heritage. This awareness has given historians a greater appreciation for our society's material culture and its importance to us as legitimate evidence of our past.

As part of our material culture, quilts have become a vehicle for interpreting our connection to the past and serve as an important cultural document reflecting both personal and community experience. They are also considered works of art. The thought, skill, and care stitched into each quilt is a testament to the human spirit of creativity. Contemporary quiltmakers share, with the thousands of quilters who came before, a strong sense of commitment to thoughtful craftsmanship and to conveying new insights and views about their world. The quilts in Visions–The Art of the Quilt are visible proof of a tradition which reaches back to our nation's earliest days and of an evolution of patterns and techniques that has established quiltmaking as one of America's truly indigenous art forms.

This extraordinary exhibition is matched by the tireless effort Quilt San Diego has expended to bring about the successful development of the Visions project. Special thanks go to Executive Director Lynn Johnson, Quilt San Diego President Diane Seaberg, and the many fine people who have worked so hard for the past two years to plan and execute every detail.

In addition to Visions–The Art of the Quilt, the Museum of San Diego History is pleased to present Always There: The African-American Presence in American Quilts. This exhibition of quilts from the 19th and 20th century surveys the full range of the African-American contribution to the mainstream of American quiltmaking. Curated by noted quilt scholar Cuesta Benberry, Always There graphically illustrates how black quilters drew inspiration from their environment and experience, and from one another. The San Diego Historical Society believes that presenting these two important exhibitions concurrently provides an opportunity for the visitor to see how each group of quiltmakers has been influenced, over time, by the other and how indistinct the lines separating them have now become.

Celebrate with us the creative spirit of individual quiltmakers in this uniquely expressive and beautiful art form.

James Vaughan
Executive Director
San Diego Historical Society

5

6

YOU CAN ALMOST HEAR IT

61″ x 61″
Cotton.
Machine piecing, machine quilting.
From the collection of Bernice M. Stone.

This is the first quilt in the "round peg from square holes" series, in which traditional blocks are placed in a circular path. This piece was designed to introduce a class of the same name, first taught at Quilt San Diego's Visions–A New Decade in 1990.

INTRODUCTION

◆

Margaret J. Miller

When, in the future, historians research the art quilting movement of the 1980s and 1990s, they will rely on the information presented in catalogs like the one you now hold in your hands. We wonder what future readers will conclude about us on the basis of the quilts found in these pages. And we hope that future quiltmakers will have access to written and pictorial documentation of even more quilts which will give further perspective to an exhibition like this one.

Researchers will find it interesting to compare artists' statements in this and other catalogs of national and international competitions occurring within the last 5 to 10 years. They will find motivation to create quilts for more than the practical purposes of warmth or protection: quilts celebrating life or mourning deceased friends; quilts representing complex emotional and psychological journeys to self-knowledge or self-acceptance; quilts making strong statements about women's issues in the current society. Studying quilts in this exhibit, they will see that many were inspired by varied causes and controversies: some react to the Gulf War of early 1991, while others are "Green Quilts" focusing our attention on the conservation of our planet. Others reveal keen senses of humor and satire.

Diverse and innovative approaches to quilt design are immediately apparent in this book. The historical and traditional roots of quiltmaking will be more recognizable in some pieces, well-hidden in others. The construction techniques found in these quilts have grown considerably from the traditional options of pieced or appliquéd, hand or machine quilted. No longer are quilts made according to rigid rules. Fabric is no longer used as a rigid geometric shape, but as a brush stroke of color on the quilt surface.

It is evident that the quiltmakers shown in these pages use a plethora of surface design techniques, both before and after the quilt is made: seam allowances are no longer relegated to interior layers of the quilt; painting techniques are explored with abandon from airbrush to rice-paste resist to controlled bleaching; photocopied images and computer-generated graphic designs are accepted design elements. Likewise, materials are not restricted to cotton and cotton/polyester blends. The fabrics which appear on these pages come from all over the world and are augmented by such "unquiltlike" materials as plastic toys, lamé, and leather.

Historians will note that quiltmakers represented here often work in series; for some artists, parts of a given series of quilts are represented in various exhibition catalogs; for others, only a single piece from a series is featured in published collections like this one. Also apparent is networking among artists and a flow of influence between the quiltmakers. A careful reading of the artists' statements reveals a familiarity with others' works. This network extends to a sharing of materials; for example, a number of pieces include hand-dyed fabrics from other artists in this group. There is an even more subtle and perhaps more vital networking represented by the publication and public sharing of this book. Some quiltmakers live in unsupportive places where their work is neither understood nor accepted. The photographs and descriptions here represent a psychological lifeline to which such quiltmakers may cling when they find little or no positive feedback.

Beyond the controversy of whether or not this grouping of quilts reflects the cutting edge of contemporary quiltmaking or whether this collection is an accurate representation of the range of quilts being created in 1992 lies the real message of this exhibit—that quiltmaking is alive and vigorous and expanding in diverse directions! As long as the pieces that individual quiltmakers submit to competitions such as this one represent personal growth, and as long as these exhibitions spur individual quiltmakers to attempt risks as artists and craftsmen, then the purposes of this competition are well-served.

DREAMING OF A ROOM OF MY OWN
94" x 75"
Hand-dyed cotton.
Traditional piecing, landscape strip piecing, hand appliqué.
Photo by Ken Wagner.

Several years ago, I took over my children's playroom as a temporary studio. Since then I've had architectural plans drawn for a wonderful studio, but neither saws nor hammers are busy on this project since my children are beginning the long college trek. So for now I must bide my time, and simply dream of a room of my own. Thus this quilt is a visual interpretation of my longing for this room. *Dreaming of a Room of My Own* also shows the progression of my work and my interests in the quiltmaking field during the past 16 years. The wallpaper is created through traditional piecing methods. The window and panes are hand appliquéd. The mountains and hills are realistically constructed by landscape strip piecing techniques. The wisteria hanging over the window and the plants growing at the bottom of the window are more abstractly created, giving an impressionistic style. Thus, this quilt is a visual tale of both my technical development and much of my quiltmaking interest to date.

8

JURORS' STATEMENTS

◆

Joen Wolfrom

As quilt artists, we each have our own sensitivity to beauty, color, scale, and design. This artistic preference to creative imagery is highly personal. The designs that appeal to us, the way we strive to put our colors together, the fabrics and textures that we choose, the techniques that we adopt—there are no rights or wrongs in these matters. Therefore, our personal form of expression must not be confined by limitations imposed by others, nor should we let the judgments of others influence our artistic direction. As the masters of our own creative voices, we should feel free to work in the area and manner that allows our unique perception and artistic spirit to emerge to its fullest extent.

Because the philosophy of the exhibit Visions—The Art of the Quilt embraces and celebrates the creative spirit of individual quilt artists throughout the world, it was not the assignment or intent of the jurors to make judgments upon the entries with regard to theme, imagery, or technique. Certainly, it was not for us to use our own personal artistic leanings to influence our decisions as to what would be included in this exhibit. Instead, our responsibility was to gather together a representative group of quilts that artistically encompass the total spectrum of contemporary quilt art. This meant that quilts of many varied styles, techniques, themes, and artistic perspectives were thoughtfully viewed and discussed several times prior to selection.

After four full days of intense viewing of the entries, we made our final selection. For a small group among these quilt artists, the results were most likely received with exuberance, as they were invited to include their work in a prestigious exhibit that thousands of viewers will enjoy. For the majority of entrants, however, the jurors' decision probably brought the opposite feeling, along with a sense that we may have made a negative judgment about their work. Entrants, however, should not view their quilt entry's exclusion from this show as a statement or reflection of their creative endeavors. With the breadth of diversity present in the quiltmakers' entries, it was imperative that we select a well-balanced range of quilt art. This, in itself, often precluded the selection of many excellent entries that were similar in style or imagery. Additionally, because the number of entries far exceeded the exhibit space, less than one in twelve entries could be selected.

With regard to artistic expression, success should not be measured by awards, publicity, fame, or inclusion in an exhibit. Instead, success is a personal interpretation of how we perceive both the process and the result of our own endeavors. It is my hope that each of you who is committed to creating innovative quilt art will remember that you are the best and most important judge of the success of your own work. Simply, after completion of a work of art, if your desired visual statement was achieved, if you were able to challenge yourself and grow during the process, if you enjoyed the various stages of work, if the end result visually pleased you, or if the work inspired you to explore further, then indeed your work was successful. To share its success with others through an exhibit such as Visions is merely icing on the creative cake.

I applaud those of you who so enthusiastically entered the Visions jurying process, and congratulate you for the courage and commitment to be so beautifully expressive. May you continue to enjoy the creativity of your art form.

10

THE BLUES DOUBLE WEDDING RING
72" x 72"
Pima cottons, hand-dyed cottons.
Piecing, strip piecing; quilting by Marie Moore.
Photo by J Kevin Fitzsimons.

This is the sixth quilt in a series based on the Double Wedding Ring pattern. My interest lies in "pushing the visual impact" by enlarging the original pattern to such big shapes that the viewer is nearly overwhelmed.

Nancy Crow

◆

I found that being asked to be one of the jurors for a major international exhibition brought out two conflicting emotions in me. On the one hand I felt honored to be included and looked forward to working with the other two jurors, but then, I began to question whether quiltmakers should be judging the work of other quiltmakers. Ideally I feel that this is a job that should be conducted by directors and curators of museums or by other experts prominent in the textile field. But sadly, there are very, very few specialists in most museums or even in textile departments around the United States who are at all knowledgeable about what is happening in contemporary quiltmaking.

Three days were spent in reviewing nearly a thousand slides. This process included viewing, debating calmly and sometimes heatedly, discussing the particular focus for Visions–The Art of the Quilt, then viewing yet again and again until the final selections were made. After this intense period of work, I felt this process was one of the most grueling experiences I have been through. The experience made me repent all my own "angry feelings" at all jurors who decided not to choose my work in the past. In many cases I think each of the jurors would have selected different quilts to be included that all three of us together could not agree upon. And so it goes.

As I looked at the slides, the criteria I used included the following: authenticity–the quilt needed to be endowed with a sense of real authority, a sense of its maker; freshness–the quilt could not be an imitation of the work of an already-famous quiltmaker; timeliness–the quilt must not look "dated," like work from the late 1970s and early 1980s. I also rejected what I perceived as nothing more than a tour de force.

Unfortunately a significant number of entries were rejected due to the poor quality of the photographs. I am emphatic on this point and urge you as quiltmakers and artists to seek the services of a highly-skilled or professional photographer to capture the importance of your work. Further, I suggest you present your quilt as it might be hung in a gallery or exhibit, not in a cluttered or overly casual background, and with sufficient light to enhance color, design, and content. Only then will a juror be able to evaluate your hard work on its true merits.

I loved working with Joen and Paul and feel we chose a show that reflects the best work from many parts of the world, not only in the art quilt movement but also in the more traditional quilt movement.

Paul J. Smith

◆

After reviewing the 953 submissions for Visions–The Art of the Quilt, I was left with strong impressions of the imagination and creativity of fiber artists of the 1990s exploring the quilt as an artistic medium. In both number and quality, the works demonstrate that quilt art represents one of the most vital areas of the contemporary fiber art field.

The Visions entries displayed the versatility that fiber artists use in approaching quiltmaking today. Many artists, having acknowledged their esthetic roots in the rich American historical tradition of quiltmaking, are exploring new horizons. If we examine the movement over the past twenty years, we see an increasing trend in innovation, and a breaking away from traditions of format and structure. A growing number of contemporary quilt artists are bringing a sense of vibrancy to surface embellishment, adding textural elements and using modern technology such as photo imagery, laser prints, and acrylic paints. The juxtaposition of these processes often adds a startling new dimension to the classic quilting format.

While most of the submissions explore the fiber esthetic and incorporate rich use of textile imagery, distinct stylistic directions do emerge. Many of the works emphasize geometric patterns, often with exciting color and illusion effects. One challenging area is found in pieces associated with contemporary art trends, although these works occasionally seem contrived as they tried to simulate stylistic trends of other media.

An intriguing aspect of quiltmaking art today is that it has become global in nature. For Visions—The Art of the Quilt there were entries from seventeen countries, and six countries are represented in the final selection. Although not singled out in the review process, the international entries could often be recognized by their ethnic spirit. Many of the foreign entries, although influenced by the American quilt tradition, reflect the fiber traditions of their own geographic areas. This is particularly true with the works from Asia, which incorporate distinctive fabric elements. This global trend is increasing in every field of contemporary creative expression, and we can look forward to further cross-cultural influences in fiber art as this international movement continues to expand.

To select seventy works from nearly a thousand entries was a monumental task. It was enjoyable to review the vast number of entries with my professional colleagues. In general, I believe we shared a common goal of selecting those works which represent overall successful and personal statements. Our additional goal was to choose the best works reflecting the broad range of stylistic directions, from traditional expression to the more avant-garde. With such a wealth of creative works from which to choose, I feel we have assembled a strong collection to celebrate the dynamic state of quilt art today!

◆

MARGARET J. MILLER
Woodinville, Washington

Ms. Miller is a contemporary studio quiltmaker who travels widely teaching color and design in quiltmaking. Author of the books *Blockbuster Quilts* and *Strips That Sizzle*, and contributor to *Quilt with the Best*, her writings and presentations are known for their enthusiasm, humor, and sincere encouragement of quiltmakers of all levels of skill and experience.

JOEN WOLFROM
Fox Island, Washington

Ms. Wolfrom is an artist, quiltmaker, teacher, lecturer, writer, mother, wife, and homemaker. Although remaining active in the educational community, Ms. Wolfrom, author of *Landscapes & Illusions* and *The Magical Effects of Color*, commits most of her time to teaching, lecturing, writing, and commission work.

NANCY CROW
Baltimore, Ohio

An organizer of Quilt National, Ms. Crow is an artist, quiltmaker, teacher, and lecturer. Considered among the most innovative of contemporary quilt artists, she is known for her use of bold patterns and strong colors in her quilt designs. Author of *Nancy Crow: Quilts and Influences*, she recently organized Quilt/Surface Design Symposium.

PAUL J. SMITH
New York, New York

Director Emeritus of the American Craft Museum in New York, Mr. Smith has received wide recognition for imaginative and creative exhibition programming. A lecturer, juror, and consultant on craft and design issues, he now oversees exhibition design and installation for the United States Information Agency, Arts America program.

THE
QUILTS

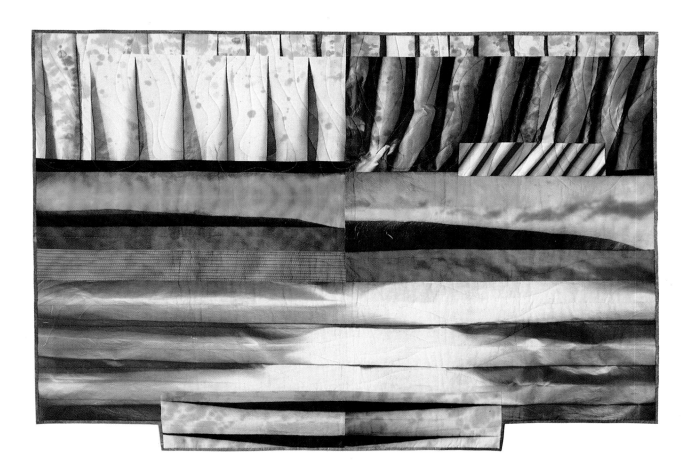

UPPER AIR DISTURBANCE
49" x 70"
Cotton, fiber-reactive dyes; polyester batting.
Painting with dyes, cyanotype, machine piecing, hand quilting.

Is this the calm before the storm, or has the storm just passed? In this seascape, color sets the mood and stripes convey the energy that draws the viewer into the scene. The stripes are printed on the dyed fabric by pleating and sunprinting. This collaboration with the sun always creates a factor of surprise. I pinched the pleats like a paper fan in the top section, made them very large in the center, and creased them in the lower area. I enjoy working with the directional element of stripes in a collage format.

16

LIFE'S RICH TAPESTRY
55" x 55"
Cotton, cotton/polyester blends, cotton overdyed by Debra Lunn, cotton designed by
Jimmy Pike (Australia), lamé, spandex, silk organza, Sulky® thread, sequins.
Machine appliqué, hand painting.

One of my husband's philosophical shrugs of the shoulder is his expression "…part of Life's Rich Tapestry." In a David Walker class on the use of personal images in quilt designs, a discussion of passages set me thinking of life as a progression; of the Rainbow Serpent, an Australian aboriginal mythological figure; and of the game Snakes and Ladders (Chutes and Ladders® in America). In the game, the throw of the dice determines one's progress, with reversals and surges forward when one lands on a snake or at the foot of a ladder. This game, like life, can be a series of cycles: when someone wins by getting to the final square, another game is often started.

On this quilt, the checkerboard (Life—the Game for Players of All Ages) is depicted with symbols representing many influences such as the elements, seasons, star signs, gender, fertility, birth and death, etc. The large golden serpent, whose head rests on the end square and tail on the beginning, represents the cyclical nature of life. The dice and the hazy wheel of fortune surround the board representing the luck of the draw. But this is not a fatalistic view of life; the chess pieces represent strategic planning. Mastery of the moves can influence all outcomes. All these symbols and influences are set against a crazy patchwork background composed of dark and light, bright and dull, ugly and pretty, touched here and there by the glitter of gold and sequins—*Life's Rich Tapestry*.

COLOURWASH STRIPES AND BLUE TRIANGLES
41″ x 64½″
Cotton, cotton blends; cotton/polyester batting.
Machine piecing, hand quilting.

For several years now I have designed quilts employing the technique of shading using commercially printed fabrics. In this piece, the first to emerge in fabric from the many ideas I have on paper, I treat shading, the "colourwash," as my background on which I lay bright flecks of color in a contrasting arrangement. The development of my work has been greatly influenced by the historical and economic traditions of quiltmaking. Scrap quilts and scraps of fabric are my delight!

26

DESERT STORM QUILT
95" x 85"
Cotton, silk, acrylic paint, smashed toy metal cars, toy plastic gas pumps, plastic skeletons,
machine embroidery thread.
Appliqué by hand and machine, reverse appliqué by hand and machine, embellishing,
painting, hand quilting by Sue Rule.

During "Desert Storm," as war images appeared daily on the TV screen and yellow ribbons embellished the country, I was torn between my desire to be patriotic and my empathy with the 100,000 human beings who were killed by our bombing. We tied our yellow ribbons around our missiles, hardly making note of the destruction of the people and environment.

The smashed cars and gas pumps represent our dependency on automobiles and oil. The body bags and skeletons represent those we killed for oil. Although I am proud of our country's technological capabilities, I would feel more pride if we had used the money and technology to develop other energy sources so we wouldn't need to be involved in this kind of war again.

BLOCK PARTY
86" x 86"

Cotton, cotton blends, rickrack, buttons, beads, ribbon, embroidery floss, metallic thread. Strip piecing, machine inlay, appliqué, embroidery, hand quilting, machine quilting, coloring with markers.

Two special fabrics inspired me to make *Block Party*. While traveling through the Yukon Territory in Canada I found the "guitar" fabric in Dawson City. A short time later I found the "penguin party" fabric. It was then that I decided to use the fabrics together to make a spontaneous, happy quilt that would express the mood of dancing and having a rollicking good time! Portions of the two multicolored blocks are machine inlaid into a gray background. Their topsy-turvy placement suggests the merrymaking one experiences at a really good party.

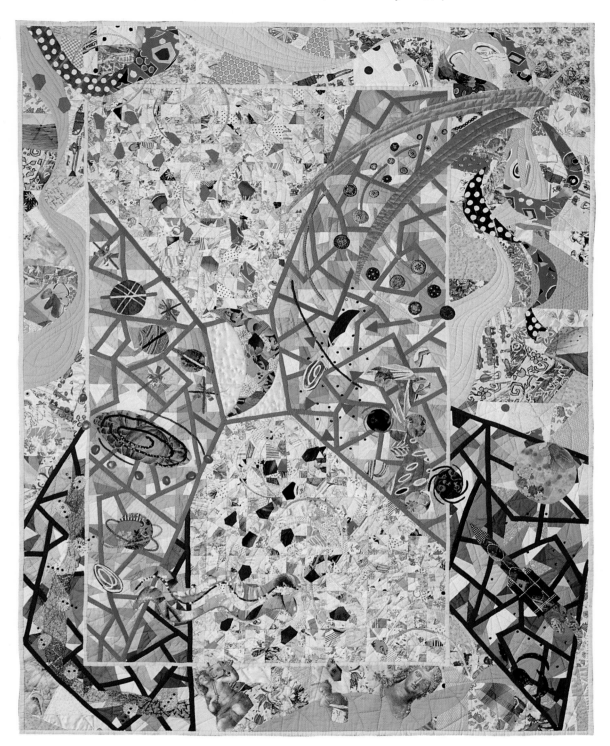

28

RIBBON STAR
71" x 55"
Cotton, sateen, silk, ribbons, sequins, embroidery floss.
Hand piecing, appliqué, embroidery.

When I look through my ribbon collections, each ribbon leads me to imagine different moods: lace ribbons take me to a romantic mood, polka dots take me to a nostalgic mood, and checkered ribbons take me back to when I was a little schoolgirl. All these images led me to design this quilt.

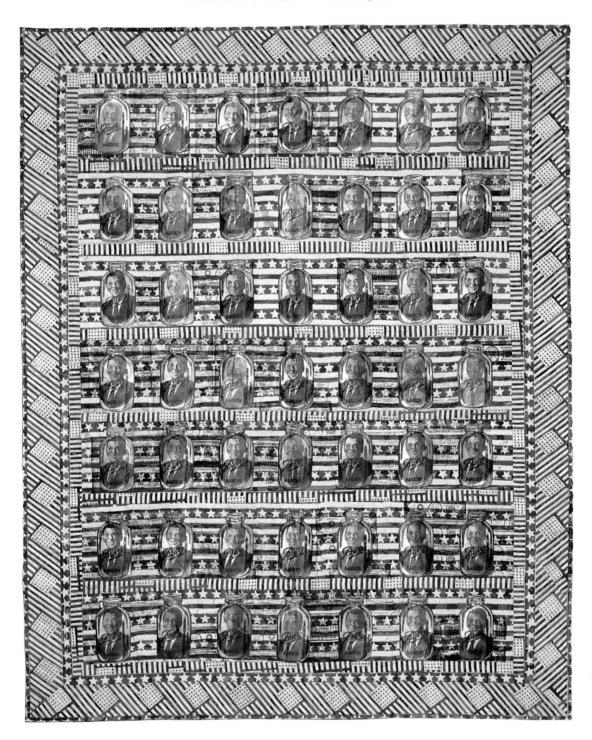

WELL PRESERVED

81″ x 61″

Cotton, polyester; cotton batting.
Silkscreening, machine piecing, machine appliqué, machine quilting.

Well Preserved is a tongue-in-cheek comment on the well-preserved good looks of former President Ronald Reagan. The repeated images of our American President are portrayed as a commodity that is packaged, preserved, and sold in the very best American tradition. I chose the Ball® Mason jar as the container for our President because it effectively seals him from contamination.

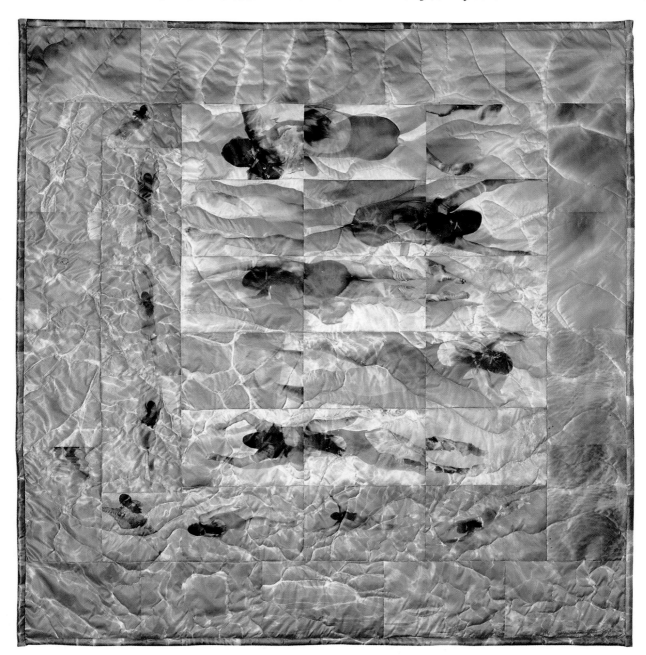

VERMONT SWIMMERS
85″ x 85″
Acetate, heat transfers.
Color photocopy transfer, machine quilting.

The rich tradition of American quiltmaking as a process of recording personal histories in cloth has inspired my work. The compilation of bits of fabric from daily life creates a kaleidoscope of memories, a documentation of life. Using my own photographs, I incorporate many personal images in my fabric pieces. These frozen moments in time lend themselves to the idea of the quilt as a diary of biographical associations.

These photographic scraps of time and texture juxtapose what is real and the image of what is real. I like to combine textural surface treatments with flat images that look dimensional, thereby creating an interplay of the tangible and the image of the tangible. The fabric of this quilt and the images printed on the fabric have similar qualities: texture, sheen, draping characteristics, and fluidity.

31

GAIA
90" x 86"
Cotton.
Stencil printing using rice-paste resist, dye painting, drawing, machine piecing,
machine quilting.

My quilt is named after Gaia, the Greek goddess of the Earth. It is dedicated
to Lynn Margulis who, with James Lovelock, formulated the theory of "Gaia's
Hand." This theory maintains that everything on the Earth is connected and that
the Earth is a self-regulating, self-maintaining system.

The primary motif on the quilt is the leaf. Within the many leaves are animals,
bugs, trees, and various other things including my cat, my house, my sister, and
myself. The quilt is made of whole cloth; the entire design is painted onto one
piece of fabric, and is neither appliquéd nor pieced. First I created a large stencil to
use in applying rice-paste resist to the fabric. Then I painted the entire piece with
dye. When I washed the fabric, those places that were blocked by the rice paste
remained white while the other areas were colored. After steaming and washing the
fabric, I dried it, then quilted it.

32

I SEE THE MOON
64" x 57"
Cotton, fabric paint, metallic and Sulky® threads, filament, permanent pen,
fiber-reactive dye.
Machine appliqué, strip piecing, string piecing, machine quilting.

I *See the Moon* incorporates many levels of personal and spiritual symbolism displayed as images of past, present, and future in the mind of the daydreamer. The "goddess graffiti" symbolizes the daydreamer's past as goddess, while the puppet, surrounded by many moons, symbolizes both the present and the child's prayer for which the quilt is named. Further, the puppet's body is made of strips which in their variety and alignment represent the future, a combination of freedom and unity.

Intentionally, this puppet has no strings attached. What autonomy! While making the quilt I did not consciously see it as a self-portrait, but now I feel it speaks for all women who dream of things past, present, and future. My special thanks for inspiration to Barbara G. Walker, Jules Olitsky, Claude Monet, Yvonne Porcella, Elizabeth Busch, and my little Puppeteers.

DRIZZLE
72" x 60"
Cotton; polyester batting.
Machine piecing, machine quilting.

Having already made two small quilts using the zigzag motif, I wanted to create a more complex design based on the same idea. *Drizzle* is the result. When I was partially through designing and cutting, it all looked muddy to me. I even labeled its storage box "Muddy Waters." As I neared the final design, I tried and discarded various water names until I came to "drizzle." I liked the idea that the shapes of the double Z's in the word mirrored the zigzags in the quilt. The finished work reminded me of one of those dark, drizzly days when all the colors are heightened by the diffused, watery light.

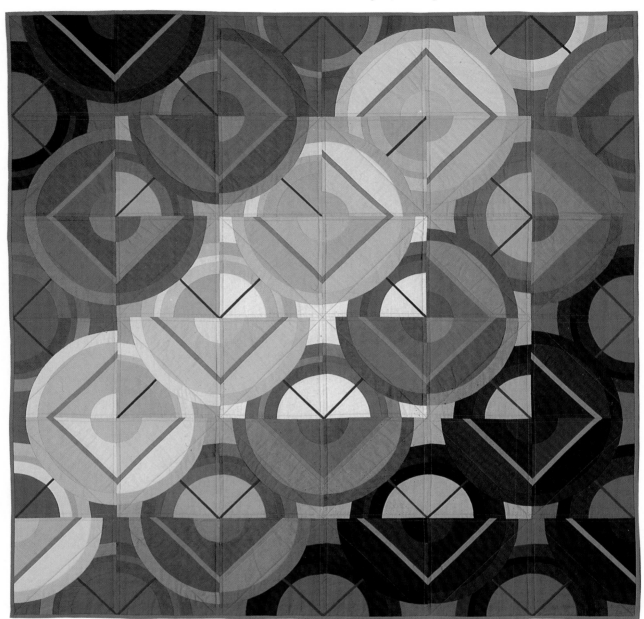

34

BROKEN CIRCLES II
60" x 60"
Hand-dyed cotton.
Machine piecing, machine quilting.

Broken Circles is one of a series of quilts using a block that I designed in 1990. It reflects my long-time fascination with curvilinear designs. *Broken Circles* is about breaking away from traditional forms, usages, and explanations.

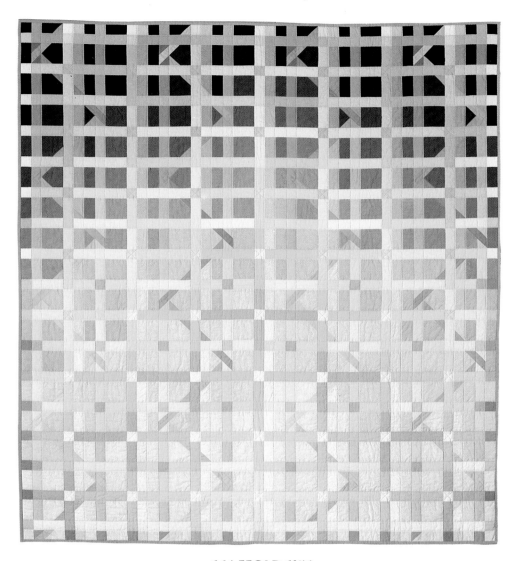

35

SCAFFOLD SKY
64" x 55"
Cotton muslin, cotton sateen, hand-dyed with Procion® dyes.
Machine piecing, machine quilting.

The idea for this quilt took shape while I observed the facelift to a neighborhood fire station. The geometric grid structure of the scaffolding especially intrigued me. At night, the areas of the scaffolding were highlighted by city lights and the building behind it became less obvious. The scene was a perfect subject to explore my fascination with spatial illusions, architectural structure, and color interactions.

I wanted my quilt "sky" to be both night and day. Against this sky background I played with spatial relationships by having parts of the scaffold either contrast or fade out. After piecing sample areas, I made a chart to determine the value progressions of each element, not knowing exactly how some areas would look. It is important to me to make some decisions and then jump into the piecing process. The piecing is less tedious when I am continuously seeing new color relationships for the first time.

In the last two years I have been dyeing my own fabric. Taking Jan Myers-Newbury's fabric-dyeing course was a turning point for me. I found the process to be fun, easy, and dependable. It also opened up the whole world of color mixing. Some of my favorite discoveries have been colors I would have passed up in a fabric store as being "too ugly."

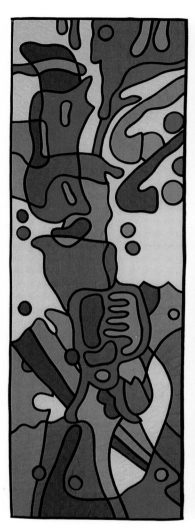

IN ANY EVENT, MR. LOTUS AND THE MAD BIRD
WILL COME TO SING

70″ x 75″
Hand-dyed cotton.
Hand appliqué, hand quilting.

Recently, after years of making precise geometric quilts, I began painting with tempera on paper, a medium that I find to be quicker, freer, and more immediate. Making no conscious effort to paint about any particular subject, I am beginning to remember and illuminate events from my childhood, dreamworld, and unconscious. Translating those paintings into fabric has resulted in a series of quilts that are bold, colorful, graphic abstractions of my life story.

In this triptych, from left to right, the figures become more identifiable as human males. They represent the male aspect of myself, a place to find a connection with the spiritual. This transformation follows my progress in a psychological and emotional journey as I am better able to define and accept myself. The figure in the left panel is an elaborately dressed, stiff soldier while the one in the center has an exposed, transparent body. The many creatures asking for help bewilder him. The rather regal figure in the right panel has his feet planted firmly on the ground, connected to the earth.

Motifs such as wavy quilting lines and strange creatures suggest the dreamworld or the unconscious. The fluid, bubbly circles give the viewer a feeling that the images will ooze into other shapes, reflecting my belief that life is a constantly changing process.

MUMBO JUMBO 1: RECURRING DREAMS
54" x 39"
Commercial cotton, hand-dyed cotton; cotton batting.
Machine piecing, hand quilting.

Studying improvisational African-American quilts, including those in the "Who'd A Thought It?" exhibit curated by Eli Leon and those by Anna Williams in Baton Rouge, Louisiana, prompted me to make this quilt. After spending most of my life designing and planning (I'm an architect as well as a quiltmaker), I wondered if I could work directly with fabric with no sketches or templates.

I began piecing triangular scraps, leftovers from many earlier quilts, into small units with no particular end result in mind. In this cluster of units, a composition began to emerge. As I proceeded, the completed portion became a "context" to which I could respond; the existing portion suggested each new step. Although the end result may seem simple and humble, this quilt required an intense level of concentration which I could sustain for only 2 to 3 hours at a time.

KITTY AND FIREFLIES IN THE BUSH
87" x 78"
Cotton, textile paint, beads, African painted fabric.
Painting, appliqué; quilting by Connie Blumberg.

This quilt design was inspired by a painting I did several years ago. This particular theme came about through my summer-evening walks in New York City parks, where there are feral cats and other animals and also shadows of humans. The night lights cause strange forms and colors to become ghostly tones. Cats running by look into the lights with shiny bead-like eyes. Before night darkens, the evening twilight provides fireflies dancing to a silent song and silhouettes beginning to move about. In the night, parks become one big bush with no distinguishing features, no trees, no flowers, and no paths. You see only "kitty and fireflies in the bush."

38

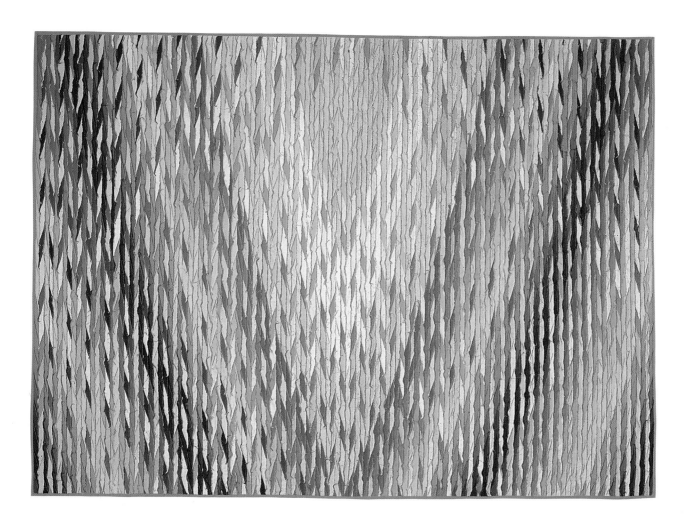

RAINBOW
69" x 89"
Hand-dyed cotton; cotton batting.
Hand dyeing, machine piecing with all seams exposed, strip piecing, hand quilting.

For me the source of inspiration and motivation for a new quilt begins with cottons that I have hand dyed. The colored textile material speaks to me in a very emotional way. In this quilt I wanted to honor the many shades of the rainbow— when sunshine starts again. With all the seams exposed the quilt gains movement and vibration.

40

AMERIFLORA I
99" x 91"
Cotton blends, acrylic paint, Shiva® paintsticks.
Machine piecing, machine appliqué, machine quilting.

At the beginning of October 1992, the 500th anniversary of Christopher Columbus's voyage, my home city will host Ameriflora '92, a grand international horticultural exhibition. This quilt, commemorating Ameriflora, is one of a series of architectural designs that I have made over the past twelve years. I hope to convey the feeling of celebrating nature.

HUNTING GAME
62½" x 45½"
Cotton canvas, purchased fabric, acrylic paint, textile ink, Prismacolor® pencil, embroidery floss, ribbon.
Hand painting, airbrush painting, silkscreening, hand appliqué, machine appliqué, hand embroidery, hand quilting.

In 1988 Donald Rogerson shot and killed Karen Wood in a tragic hunting accident in Hermon, Maine, about ten miles from where I live. Wood was in her backyard. Rogerson had a "bucks only" permit. Wood wore white mittens...but no antlers. Rogerson was acquitted of manslaughter in 1990.

My fears of the hunting season while my children grew erupted at the news of this acquittal, and memories of hunting accidents and the dread of those days were stirred once again. Our neighbor's horse was shot to death by a hunter; once bullets whizzed by my head while I was pruning our backyard raspberries; my children waited in fluorescent vests for the school bus and did not play in the yard during hunting season. The beautiful deer that visited our back fields in summer were now in a panic, as was I.

While at the Banff Centre for the Arts, Alberta, Canada, in the fall of 1990, I developed a ten-piece body of work regarding the Rogerson/Wood incident. *Hunting Game* is the first piece in that series.

42

HEXAGON
84½" x 84½"
Chirimen silk.
Hand piecing, hand quilting.

The fabric of this quilt came from an old Chirimen silk kimono, a garment usually worn by a woman of noble birth. As I enhanced the beautiful color and texture of the silk, I used the hexagon motif to show the design flow from the center of the quilt to the edge, which is silk from an old obi sash.

JUNKO SAWADA ◆ *Yokohama, Japan*

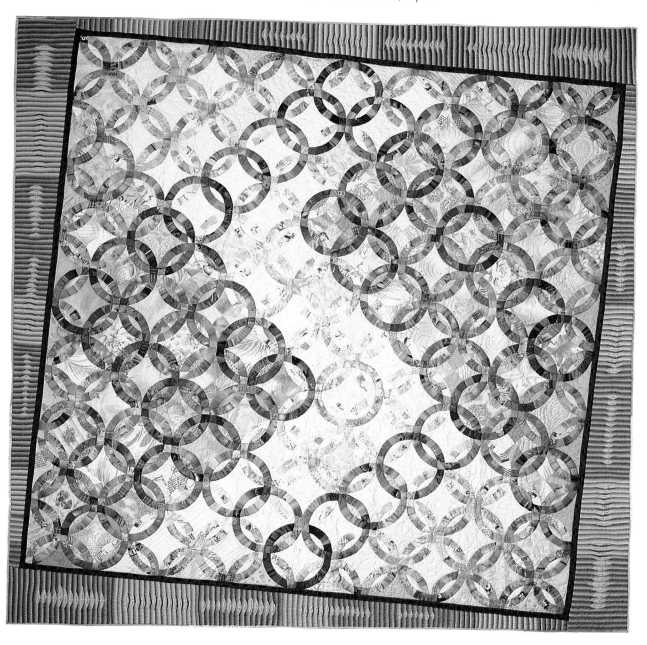

SAZANAMI (WATER RING)
86½" x 86½"
Cotton, synthetic fabric.
Hand piecing, hand quilting.

June is the wet season in Japan and also the season of hydrangeas. Azure or purple flowers are reflected in a pool of water under a gray sky. I pictured the mirrored image of hydrangeas metamorphosed into colorful water rings by sudden raindrops. The variation of lightness and brightness has a stereoscopic effect on the image of repeated water rings.

44

THE GIRL WHO HAD TO WAIT TILL SHE WAS TWENTY-ONE TO OWN A SLINKY

46" x 53"
Fabric, paint, leather, glass beads, jewelry, Slinky®.
Hand appliqué, machine appliqué, hand beading, hand quilting, machine quilting, tooled and painted leather, bottle-applied painting.

Just before she turned 21, our daughter Gretchen informed us that we had never given her a Slinky. Deprived child! We knew we'd have to make amends with a grand present for this special birthday—her own genuine Slinky! Voilà, a quilt title appeared. On our next visit to her at Kent State, we saw so many visuals in her house that the quilt took form before our eyes. An art history major and deprived daughter of crazed artists, she collects wonderful objects, including vintage hats.

Everything in this quilt is metaphoric—a loving, lively portrait of a wonderful twenty-one-year-old at college—from her hats to friends, from her cat to mice. Written all over the quilt are explanations of her story, the twenty-one-year evolution of our relationship with our very favorite person. A strong, independent, loving and playful flavor manifests itself in Gretchen's environment. A joy to experience. We hope that in the future Gretchen stays as fresh, creative, and full of life as she is now. Surrounded by good friends, maintaining a 3.91 grade point average and owning her own Slinky at last, she's well-prepared for adult life!

PATRIOT'S MAZE
59″ x 59″
Commercial fabrics, silkscreen ink.
Machine piecing, silkscreening, machine inlay, hand quilting.

This is part of a quilt series concerning the idea of mazes. There are many themes that contributed to this finished quilt. Some of the significant ideas that I considered while I conceived *Patriot's Maze* were McCarthyism, the Gulf War, and attacks on artists, homosexuals, and the National Endowment for the Arts. In part, this quilt gives a visual form to some of my concerns on these subjects.

46

HEAD SERIES VI – JOIE DE VIVRE
100" x 51"
Cotton.
Hand painting, machine piecing, machine appliqué, machine quilting.

This quilt is the sixth in a series that explores psychological growth and inner emotions. *Joie de Vivre* depicts me when I was seven months pregnant with my third son, Clark Thomas. This self-portrait celebrates the zesty fullness of motherhood and the universal richness in experiencing the cycles of birth and life on earth.

COLOR RHYTHMS
80″ x 68″
Cotton; polyester batting.
Machine piecing, hand quilting.

Because my second love, next to quiltmaking, is music (I play violin with a community symphony), I wanted to make a quilt in which the design and color reflect some aspect of music. As I auditioned colors for my repeat block, I wanted them to change with each row, yet retain the essential flow of the design. The colors became a sort of theme with variations. In each row some elements remain the same while others change. Some colors harmonize with those next to them while others are a jarring discord. The colors, as they move across and down the quilt, enhance this rhythm and give it life. Even though the colors move and change, the basic design of the quilt, the basic rhythm, remains and becomes the most important element.

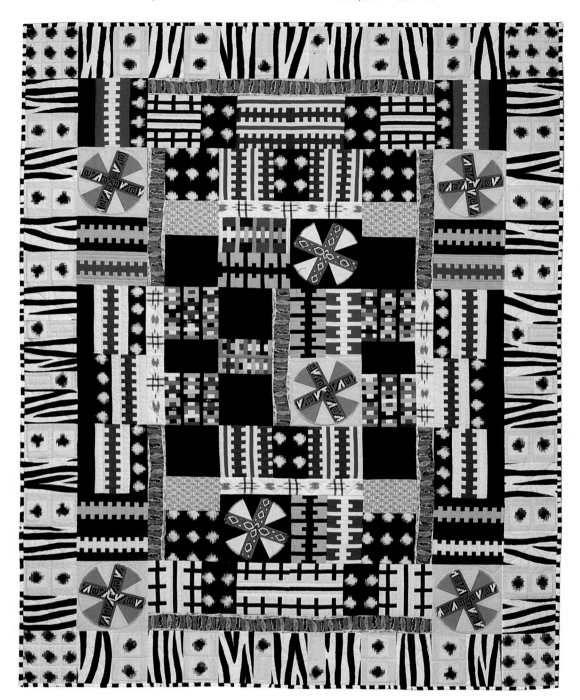

48

TRANSITIONS VII - THE GREAT ESCAPE
75" x 59"
Cotton.
Machine piecing, machine appliqué; hand quilting by Sarah Porreca.

While working on this quilt during the winter of 1990-91, I experienced a sense of being trapped. My life seemed to be pulling me in all directions. The trap was in not knowing how to avoid being pulled apart. I wanted big chunks of time for my quilt work, but I could get only a few hours here and a few hours there. The major portion of this quilt appears to be a maze: little dead-end roads, revolving doors, tiny compartments, vast areas of darkness. Freedom comes at the border of the quilt. When I designed the border and completed the quilt, I felt a great sense of relief. The door of the trap opened and I escaped!

THE GUARDIAN
67″ x 60″
Cotton; cotton batting.
Appliqué, reverse appliqué, painting, rubber stamping, airbrushing, embellishing, machine quilting.

This quilt was a spontaneous design. After deciding to work with black and gold, I played with shapes on a black background. These shapes began to take on elements like pyramids, snakes, an ankh, or a peace sign, which brought to mind both the Middle East and the 1960s. It occurred to me that the similarities remain today. The struggle still exists for equality and human rights, regardless of race, religion, gender, and political beliefs.

50

WEDDING QUILT: BOUND BY TRADITION
93" x 73"
Cotton, silk organdy; cotton batting.
Air brushing, hand painting, silkscreening, freezer-paper piecing, machine piecing, machine
embroidery, machine quilting.

In my life, the past two and one-half years have given birth to two children, discipline, social activism, and artistic freedom. Although parenthood, structure, and isolation have tested my resolve, they have been great teachers. *Wedding Quilt: Bound by Tradition* honors one of these transformations. It is my view that the traditional marriage exerts the expectation that women give all their power over in the marriage union: women are the possessions of men; women are property, not people. It is my hope that women find courage to own their freedom, within the union of marriage or not.

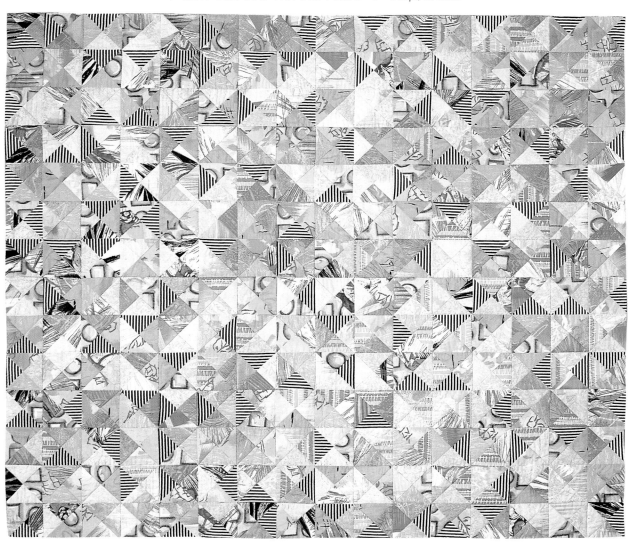

SOUTHWEST II: A GREEN QUILT
58½" x 67½"
Cotton; cotton batting.
Machine piecing, machine quilting.

I challenged myself to combine black and white fabrics with "barely there" colors, neutrals and naturals, in one quilt. Randomly piecing the fabrics, I chose the Broken Dishes pattern for its potential of motion and movement. The vibrations that come from combining the black and white stripe with the pale desert colors remind me of desert heat waves.

Each of my quilts is a challenge that satisfies my hunger for beauty, color, form, and texture. I reflect my native Dutch heritage by crossing boundaries through innovative use of traditional American patchwork. As well I want to share emotion in my quilts, whether religious, personal, or universal. I accept as my Christian vocation the charge in Genesis for us to be "stewards of the Earth," which inspires me to make "Green Quilts," representing my environmental concern expressed in a positive, open-ended way.

Respecting the fragile and hostile desert environment is crucial for survival in the Southwest, where water is a precious resource. In this series, I share my concern about the ever-increasing demand for water by the rapidly growing Phoenix area.

BLUE HORIZON
72" x 72"
Cotton, hand-dyed cotton; polyester batting.
Machine piecing, hand quilting.

This is the second in a series of three quilts, all having the illusion of depth in what is basically a two-dimensional piece of art. To give the quilts this feeling of depth, I use the contrast between light and dark to create different planes. The ombré blue and green fabrics further this effect and the quilt takes on a subtle flow. Illusion is the name of the game!

HE LOVES ME, HE LOVES ME NOT
71" x 61"
Cotton, hand-dyed muslin, craft paint.
Hand painting, machine piecing, hand quilting.

While browsing through my stash of strange but lovable fabrics, I discovered two that created music together—loud and raucous to be sure, but wonderful things happened. I grabbed my favorite book, the Gutcheons' *Quilt Design Workbook*, opened it to one of my favorite patterns, Skewed Checkerboard, and about ten minutes later began *He Loves Me*. I had to trade a print for two hand-dyed muslins; other fabrics were "I love you" gifts from dear friends. It was the quickest quilt I've ever made because it was exciting and fun from start to finish.

54

A+: MY DAUGHTER THE GLASSBLOWER
59" x 55"
Cotton; cotton/polyester batting.
Machine piecing, hand quilting.

A long history of alphabet quilts exists in the folk-craft tradition. Most were baby quilts made for warmth, love, and teaching. The history of *A+: My Daughter the Glassblower* started with my daughter's senior art show for her Bachelor of Fine Arts at Alfred University. Throughout the gallery she arranged multi-colored hand-blown glass heads on tall poles with wall pieces of glass based on Chinese pictographs. The multi-colored fabric of the A's in this quilt reminds me of the glass colors. I chose the words around the edge for personal reasons. The words are ark (moms always want to protect, provide a refuge), anxiety (where will she ever find a job glassblowing?), affirmation (you're a great kid; talented, too), absolute (follow your dreams), alphabet (keep learning through life), and amulet (we all need lucky charms).

REFRACTION #1, #2, #3
38" x 119"
Cotton; cotton batting.
Hand dyeing, machine piecing, machine quilting.

Refraction is the bending of light as it passes through a crystal. This piece is about luminescence, or light emerging from dark. My use of fabrics dyed in both chromatic and value gradations creates the illusion of luminescence. The construction is based on the traditional Log Cabin quilting technique, but it is built upon a hexagon rather than a square. The angling of each successive strip of fabric produces the illusion of the bending or spiraling of the light areas. Each panel differs slightly in composition and color and is meant to interact with the design of the adjacent panel.

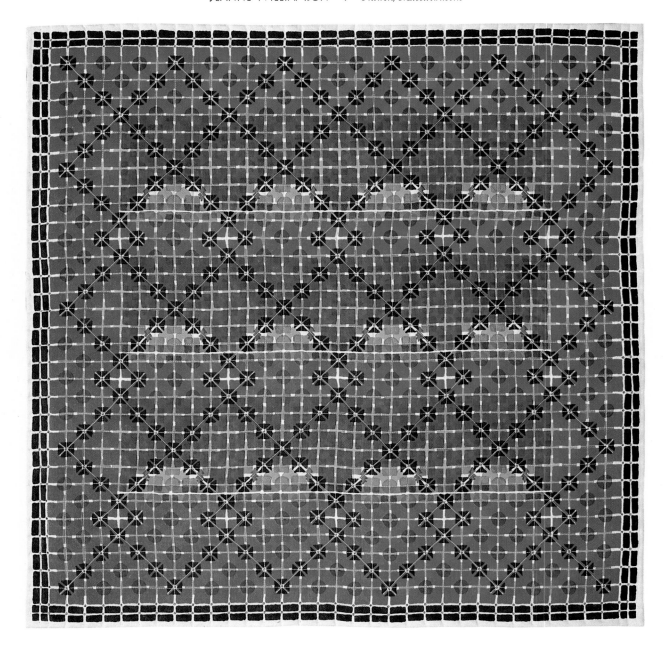

56

DUSK
40½" x 40"
Cotton, Deka® fabric paint.
Hand stamping with rubber erasers, machine quilting.

Colorful New England sunsets motivated me to make this quilt. I am very interested in Amish quilt design and used that simplicity as a starting point. After hand stamping a base grid of three bands and the red background, I added layers of orange, yellow, pink, and blue which combine to suggest the colors of a beautiful sunset. The black overlay suggests silhouettes of branches contrasted against the sky at dusk.

GREAT MOTHER TOTEMS
65" x 50"
Cotton, blends, dyes, pigments.
Screen printing, discharge printing, hand appliqué, reverse appliqué, machine piecing, hand quilting.

My work concentrates on issues relating to women. *Great Mother Totems* is the first in a series of quilts that explore from a feminist point of view the traditional role of woman as wife, mother, and nurturer. I use a photographic image of a prehistoric Great Mother figurine from Sardinia, Italy, to show women as sexual objects: it is faceless and limbless, emphasizing the breasts and body. It comes from a time when procreation was vital to the continuation of the human race. Women of today struggle to expand or, in many cases, break away from this traditional role.

My work repeats, stacks, and encloses the "women" in houses which symbolize shelter, safety, and security—the things mothers provide for their children. In another quilt in the series these houses look more like temples and become temples of love. From my viewpoint these enclosures act as traps or cages which isolate women from the rest of the world. I insert a ladder-like element at the bottom of each piece in the series to symbolize the possibility of a spiritual or physical escape.

18

EVENING SONG (SIX OF RODS I)
57½" x 72"
Cotton, blends, metallic fabric, dyed fabric, metallic and acrylic yarns, beads, sequins, fabric paint.
Machine appliqué, machine piecing, hand quilting, machine quilting.

Celebrations are joyous occasions for sharing the good news of personal achievement and creative breakthrough. The best celebrations transport us outside earthly time into places where all things become possible, where human energy is boundless, where the human spirit expands and encircles universal understanding. Sweetest are those celebrations that follow long, frustrating, seemingly non-creative periods in our lives. One lesson that we learn during these difficult times is that art inspires in many ways, and that one way is the journey through darkness. Once our creativity has regained consciousness, it seems not only natural but also imperative to embrace our achievement and celebrate our personal victory.

CELEBRATION
56" x 58½"
Cotton; cotton, metallic, and rayon threads.
Machine piecing, machine appliqué, machine quilting.

In order to force myself away from my preconceived notions of quilt design and construction, I began with African Kanga fabric whose colors I don't even usually like. Working intuitively, I cut into the fabric to see where it would take me. The result, *Celebration*, is a burst of energy and a celebration of life and its cycles, of myself and my own internal combustion, and of my life in general and all that it encompasses.

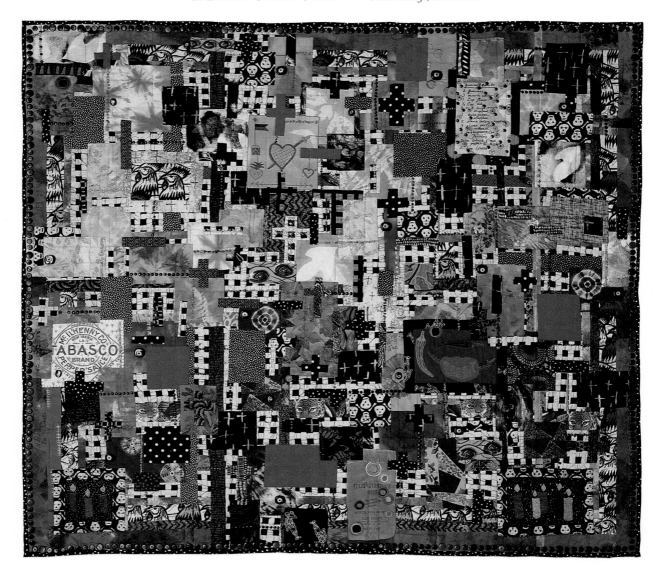

20

GUINEA GUMBO
57½" x 64"
Cotton, cotton blends, embroidery floss, shisha mirrors, beads, gemstone chips, coconut rondels, fabric paint.
Dyeing, machine piecing, hand appliqué, reverse appliqué, hand embroidery, hand quilting, beading.

Feathers and a recipe. The beginning of a quilt? A gift from a house guest—a paper bag filled with guinea-fowl feathers—and the subsequent discovery of a recipe for guinea gumbo in a Natchitoches, Louisiana, cookbook inspired me to make this quilt. (Look for the recipe on the quilt.) While I made this piece partly as a memorial to my friend's guinea-fowl flock, most of which were killed by neighborhood dogs last summer, *Guinea Gumbo* also took on its own celebratory feeling as it began to reflect Louisiana culture and food.

PERENNIAL GARDEN

52" x 45"

Commercial cotton, hand-dyed cotton, hand-painted cotton; cotton batting.
Machine piecing, hand quilting, machine quilting.

During a gray, dreary winter week not long ago, I missed the view from my kitchen window of my perennial bed with its ever-changing colors and green flora. The mood prompted me to paint the fabric for *Perennial Garden*. Working in an improvisational manner to make this quilt, I constructed the Log Cabin blocks by just cutting and sewing odd pieces of fabric.

22

THE DANGLING CONVERSATION

51½" x 57½"
Cotton muslin, dyed with Procion® fiber-reactive dyes; polyester batting.
Hand dyeing, tie dyeing, machine piecing, machine quilting.

The manipulation of color to create the illusion of three-dimensional space is a continuous theme in my work, but in the past few years I have responded to color in a more emotional way as well. The screaming yellow-green squares, for instance, could not be any other color. I tried other colors, but none had the visual or gut-level impact.

I have made perhaps 150 quilts that use the simple square (or rectangle) as the building block for the design, so in that respect *The Dangling Conversation* is from my longest on-going series. Color has always been the workhorse in my quilts.

HERB GARDEN
89″ x 89″
Cotton.
Hand piecing, hand quilting.

Imagining an herb garden with blooming rosemary and lavenders, I made this original block from the Olympia and Star Flower patterns. The different colors create a three-dimensional effect of light and shadows.

24

PRIMAL IV
47" x 62"
Commercial cotton, hand-dyed cotton, beads; cotton/polyester batting.
Machine piecing, machine quilting.

The Primal series began with a block designed with sixteen unrepeated curved pieces. *Primal I* used nine of these blocks with sashing separating the blocks in the traditional manner. In the second of the series, *Primal II*, the sashing was removed and any horizontal or vertical straight lines were eliminated through the use of color, curved cut-throughs, and quilting/surface design.

Primal III is the result of enlarging the block to a 4' x 5' format. *Primal IV*, a "Green Quilt" dedicated to the preservation of the Earth, is another version of this format. There is a landscape-like quality to this bright, swooping design where curving lines carry one across the surface. For me there is great joy and freedom in the design and process of this medium. It is always new and challenging, and the result is often surprising.

HOME FIRES BURNING
95" x 106"
Hand-dyed cotton, silk, corduroy, rayon, metallic mesh.
Machine piecing, appliqué, quilting with machine drawing.

Home Fires Burning is one of a series of night-time gardens. It's large because it's a place, a place with an inside, an outside, and a no-man's land. The piece takes its name from an old patriotic song that exhorted "the folks back home" during a war to "keep the home fires burning." The words of the song conflate the ideas of continuing a normal life and of supporting loved ones who are involved in killing during a war. One always wants to support the loved one, but may not want that support to include the actual wartime activities.

There is a terrible disjunction in our political (and personal) thinking which I find embodied in "Desert Storm" rhetoric. No one says, "War is killing and 100,000 people are now dead"; instead, they say there is "collateral damage." Inflammatory, self-righteous rhetoric and the language of obfuscation isolate us from each other and from the consequences of personal and political action. Of necessity, our sense of reality and our interconnectedness become part of the collateral damage. *Home Fires Burning*, despite its size and flamboyance, is a rather covert meditation on the personal isolation and complicity I feel when I hear those words.

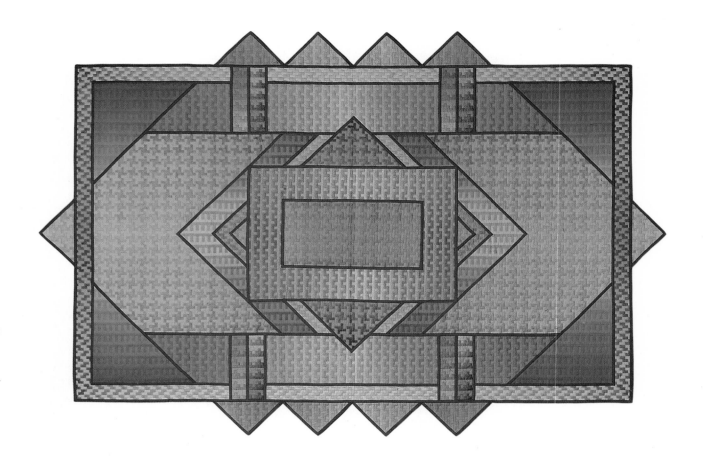

58

DEDICATION: FROM A NEW GENERATION
72″ x 108″
Cotton; cotton batting.
Hand dyeing, hand stenciling, machine piecing, machine quilting.

This quilt is my response to traditional quilts that utilize faded printed clothing fabrics. Here, I echo that fading through my fabric dyeing and stencil patterns which, in this quilt, are derived from pattern drafts of plain-weave color effects. My attraction to weaving, woven structures, and the geometry of Art Deco designs also influences the composition of this quilt.

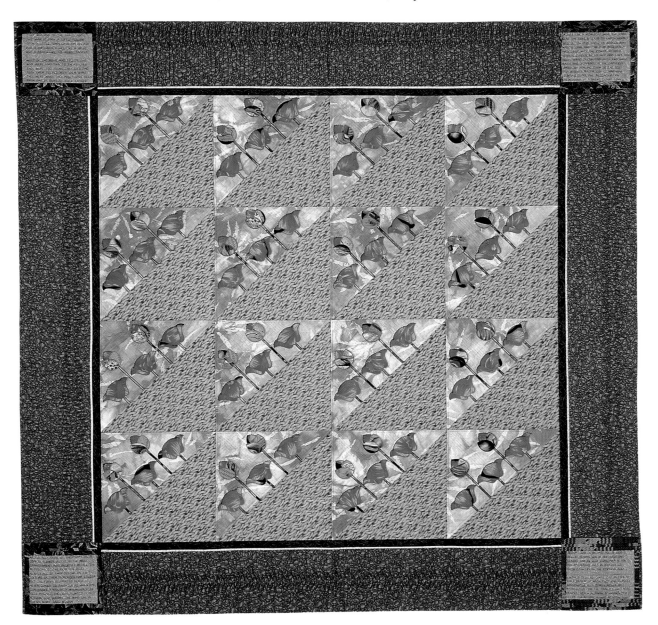

POPPIES IN THE SAND
75" x 75"
Cotton, ribbons; cotton/polyester batting.
Machine appliqué with satin and decorative stitching, couching, strip pleating, machine embroidery.

This is the second quilt in a series about people who die in war. For the first quilt I designed a 14" poppy block in tribute to soldiers in the Vietnam War. I set the symbolic red poppies on a gray background. The lower right half of the block is pleated black print fabric representing the Vietnam Memorial in Washington D.C. I named that block Poppies on the Wall.

When war in the Persian Gulf began, I decided to make another quilt using the same block, but this time I set the poppies in "sand." No two flowers are alike. On close inspection they appear to blow in the breeze, yet from a distance they line up in rows, as do the crosses at Arlington National Cemetery.

There are quotes and information in the cornerstones that are connected to the visual concept. The back label is appliquéd with a single white poppy. White, the symbol of peace, contrasts with the red poppies on the front.

60

RELEASE
86" x 76"
Cotton, cotton/polyester blends, hand-dyed and painted fabrics; cotton batting.
Machine piecing, machine quilting.

As frequently happens, this quilt took on a life of its own. Originally planned to be much smaller, the piece grew as I resolved the color-shading challenges. In addition to the use of color, structural design elements help to achieve the illusion of layers and depth. *Release* conveys both a physical explosion of energy as well as an emotional closure to a project which gives the maker the freedom to move on.

RADIANT MOMENT
92″ x 90¾″
Silk, cotton, corduroy, organdy, obi silk.
Hand piecing, machine piecing, appliqué, crazy quilting, free-hand quilting.

Whatever people do, if they do it with all their might, I am impressed. I want always to remember to do my best to create a quilt which will radiate my deep emotion. I used vivid reds and the crazy-quilt technique to fabricate my favorite flower, the rose.

62

TECHNIQUE REBELLION II
52½" x 52½"
Procion®-dyed cotton, fusible interfacing, rayon and cotton machine embroidery thread;
cotton batting.
Heat-bonded appliqué, machine embroidery, machine quilting.

Part of a series, this design is my personal symbol, a nonchalant nine-patch. It is a casual combination of my painting background and my enthusiasm for quiltmaking. The title refers to the fact that I am rebelling against traditional technique in quiltmaking: for example, I do not turn the edges under for appliqué. A nine-patch made without patchwork, heavy machine embroidery, and quilting by machine are all acts which are considered non-conformist, and that I as a quilt rebel want to do!

GINGKO WAVE
47" x 47"
Cotton, hand-dyed and painted silk; cotton batting.
Hand painting, hand dyeing, English piecing, appliqué.

Surging water cresting to become waves inspired me to do the *Gingko Wave* quilt series. Immense forces, massive gravitational pulls of the sun and the moon cause the movement of the wave itself. The very gravity of the universe is grand and never-ending. But close-up I can be in the wave. It lifts and carries objects, flowing through everything in its path.

64

POOL
41" x 41"
Cotton, cotton/polyester, cotton/rayon; polyester batting.
Hand dyeing, machine piecing, hand appliqué, machine quilting.

Watching the patterns made when a stone is dropped into water, I am intrigued by the small waves resonating out from the entry point. The waves cross each other, find an edge, and bounce back. In previous quilts I have used lines to express various kinds of motion. In *Pool*, the lines echo the circular wave movements of water.

POLYCHROME PASS
69" x 57"
Cotton muslin, gauze, organdy, fabric paint; cotton/polyester batting.
Monoprinting with fabric paint, hand painting, machine piecing, machine quilting.

In my travels one of the most beautiful places I've experienced is Denali National Park in Alaska. I have been there many times, yet I am always in awe of its beauty. Its colors linger in my memory. In this quilt, I capture the park's colors, which range from the dark greens of the spruce trees to the reds of the tundra, and on to the many colors of Polychrome Pass with its brilliant sunsets.

NO VACANCY
52" x 65"
Cotton, cotton blends.
Machine appliqué, machine piecing, machine quilting.
From the collection of Captain and Mrs. David M. Stembel, Jr.

In the time before generic chain motels lined the interstates, smaller "Mom and Pop" motels dotted the well-traveled highways. While the rooms all had a utilitarian sameness in furnishings (bed, chair, dresser and, if you were lucky, a TV), the personality was evident in the decor. Each room possessed its own unique and frequently tacky character.

This quilt is a collective memory of those motel rooms of earlier decades. The title *No Vacancy* alludes to the fact that although each quilt block is cut from an identical pattern, each room has one added sign of individual occupancy, ranging from a suitcase in the corner to a bikini swimsuit laid out on the bed.

...AND A GOOD TIME WAS HAD BY ALL
69" x 60"
Cotton and silk noil (most hand-dyed by Eric Morti), Guatemalan cotton, sateen, novelty
yarns, silk thread, perle cotton.
Fabric collage, hand appliqué, hand quilting, hand fraying, tying.

This was the beginning of my own challenge series, the primary focus being
"just do it." Whatever it is, just do something. No more procrastinating or excuses! I
have always thought this quilt should be subtitled "Yes, Virginia, there really are
miracles!" The truly amazing thing is that miracles often occur when you're feeling
"down and out," or lost, or frustrated. When things look the bleakest, there it is!

This is my miracle quilt. While working, I felt joy after extreme anxiety. I gave
myself pep talks: "Don't sweat the small stuff, Nina, just get on with it. Don't try so
hard. Things will come together if you let them." I'm still working on this last part!

It is difficult to talk about the personal nature of my quilts. What matters more
to me is not that people know my main intent, but that they feel something when
they see a particular quilt of mine.

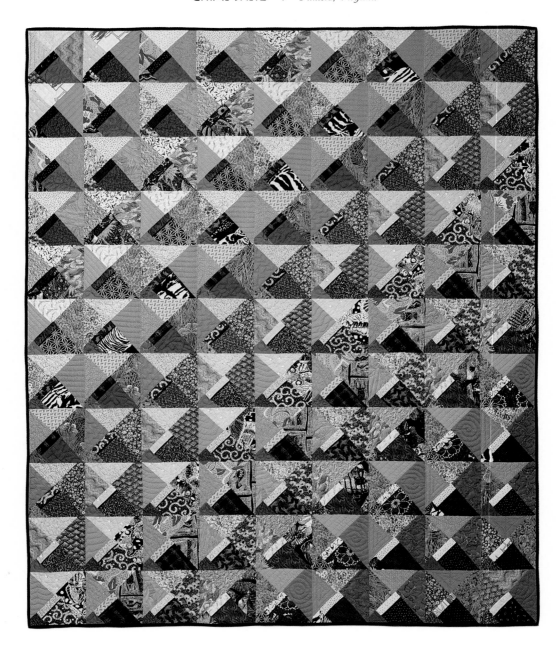

IN THE BLEAK MIDWINTER
85" x 71"
Cotton, acrylic yarn; polyester batting.
Machine piecing; hand quilting by Wendy Crigger.

In the Bleak Midwinter is a value study based on a straight setting of a block I originally designed as a participant in a "Quilt in a Series" class with Nancy Crow at Arrowmont School of Arts and Crafts in Gatlinburg, Tennessee. I completed four 16-block studies in neutrals, solids, prints, and "designer" fabrics.

Following that formal study, I drafted the entire setting and selected the fabrics. I deliberately chose black, white, and gray because they have the strongest value contrast. The absence of hue also forces the fabric to sustain the structure of the design.

The quilt title is from Christina Rossetti's "A Christmas Carol." The viewer is welcome to attribute all the bleak and dreary characteristics of winter to my quilt, but I prefer to think of the light and life surrounding Christ's birth during the winter solstice.

CALIFORNIA
83" x 94"
Cotton.
Appliqué, strip piecing, controlled bleaching, ink work, hand quilting.

In the fertile valleys of California, where I spent my childhood, there was an abundance of fresh fruits. The memory of the wonderful colors, textures, and tastes inspired me while I was making this quilt. It is my tribute to the great bounty of the Golden State.

KIM'S QUILT / THE PROTECTION OF WINGS
90" x 70"
Cotton, cotton blends.
Machine piecing, hand quilting.

In May of 1990 an old friend, Kim Cole, died. Three years had passed since I had seen her, yet her image and a flood of vivid memories immediately returned when I heard the news of her death. My tribute to her is *Kim's Quilt / The Protection of Wings*. It reflects her strength and enthusiasm, her wild and energetic nature, and, above all, her rich and nurturing spirit. This piece is intended as a covering of symbolic protection, in much the same way as a bird's feathered wings shield its young before they can take flight.

THE BLACK AND BLINDED BIRDS OF NIGHT
64" x 55"
Hand-printed cotton, textile paint, batik and block-printed Indian and African fabrics;
cotton/polyester batting.
Relief printmaking, machine piecing, hand quilting.

My work rarely reflects a single event or subject, drawing instead on my total experience of life: family, nature, music, literature, history, New York City. I find visual inspiration everywhere, from old Indian block prints to catalogues. For years my quilts were abstract with little or no representational imagery. When I began to study printmaking in 1989 my quilts suddenly exploded with colors, symbols, and patterns that are the foundation of my visual vocabulary. For this quilt I chose images that for me symbolize courage and determination. The title is from James Thompson's *The Seasons* set to music by Franz Joseph Haydn: "To dusky caverns fly the black and blinded birds of night; their moaning ghostly cries distress the anguish'd heart no more."

72

CATTYWAMPUS
60" x 60"
Cotton, cotton blends, fusible interfacing.
Machine piecing, machine satin-stitch appliqué, machine quilting.
From the collection of Joan Mason.

We are close friends with very different design styles and color sense, but with a common love of color. This is our first collaboration, begun at the suggestion of a mutual friend. We planned the quilt with a two-color, formal, graded background over which we could freely apply informal shapes. We pooled our fabrics, drew some simple shapes together to establish a sense of scale, and then went home to "play." Rebecca worked on the purple panels, Marion on the yellow. We exchanged panels as we worked, sharing shapes, inspiration, and appreciation. *Cattywampus* (meaning slantwise) was the contemporary opportunity quilt for the East Bay Heritage Quilters' show "Voices in Cloth."

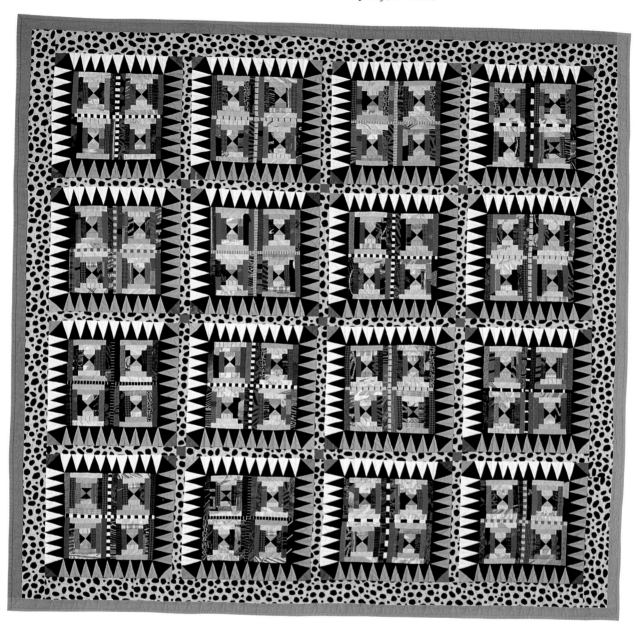

PHOENIX
74½" x 74½"
Cotton; polyester batting.
Machine piecing, hand quilting.

I made this quilt after the death of my closest friend Noreen, a talented quiltmaker. It is a very emotional piece for me, a sort of coming out of the depression after her death. Yet, in a way, it is also a celebration. The phoenix is a symbol of immortality, the triumph of life over death. The starting point in the design was the yellow leopard-spot fabric that I love.

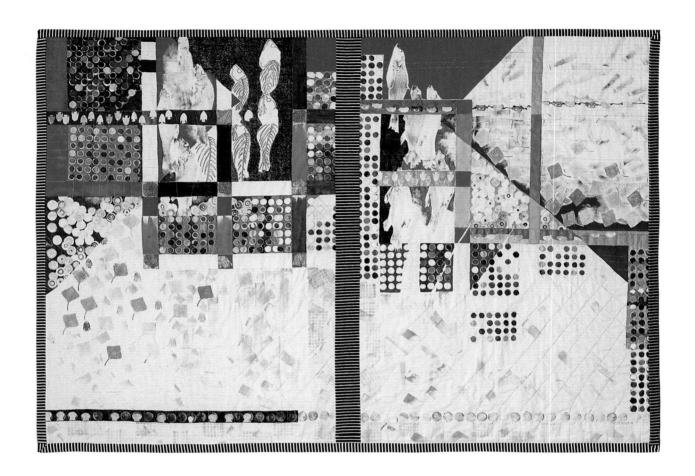

GHOST FISH RISING #2
45" x 63"
Hand-painted cotton, textile pigments.
Hand printing with real fish, rubber stamping, machine stitchery, machine quilting.

Ghost Fish Rising #2 is part of the Ghost Fish series, referring not only to my love of the ocean but also to my concern for the environmental issues of our planet. Intentionally visually pleasing, the integrated images are meant to provoke the observer to think. The combination of abstract and realistic images with an emphasis on design and color is typical of my work. *Ghost Fish Rising #2* is a "Green Quilt" dedicated to the health of our planet Earth.

THE CHILD WITHIN
100″ x 68″
Variety fabrics, found objects, buttons, sequins, lace, fabric paint, beads.
Hand piecing, machine piecing, appliqué, hand quilting, machine quilting.

Initially *The Child Within* was inspired by a friend's pregnancy, but on a deeper symbolic level the pregnant woman is the Goddess herself, set against the full moon and tied to the earth through the roots of the tree. The child resting on her swollen stomach is the "dark" child within each of us, the child that we must discover and learn to love in order to become whole. Dancers surround Her in the cycles of life and death, the Earth, the Goddess, our mother.

FIRESTORM
83" x 73½"
Japanese handwoven tosan stripes, domestic cottons, metallic thread, cotton hand-dyed or
treated by Akai Kawamoto (Japan), Debra Lunn, and Caryl Bryer Fallert; cotton/polyester
batting.
Machine piecing, machine quilting; on the back: hand appliqué, raw-edge machine appliqué,
machine piecing.

When the disastrous October 1991 East Bay fire occurred I was working on a simple striped quilt cut from my collection of Japanese tosan fabrics. The fabrics were pinned to my design wall in an overall zigzag pattern and I was contemplating which fabrics to use to fill in the diamonds to complete the quilt top. Because the project was lacking "soul," I was frustrated. In the middle of the night I realized that I had fabric in a color-run from smoky red to black. I knew then I would make the quilt a memorial of the fire. I expanded my fabric selection to include "fire" fabrics along with others depicting sky, wind, and eucalyptus leaves.

Two of my long-time quilt friends lost their homes and quilts in the blaze. On the back I wanted to mourn the lost quilts and creativity. Hands are important to a quilter, so I selected them to symbolize this loss.

76

77

MESA SKY
65" x 63"
Cotton sateen, velveteen, satin, cotton broadcloth.
Hand dye-painting, machine piecing, machine quilting, hand surface stitching.
From the collection of Tonya Littman.

This quilt interprets a summertime sunset I saw in Santa Fe, New Mexico. It is part of a series depicting various skies. Some are real, like this one, but others exist only in my imagination.

78

SPACE TRAVEL
41" x 41"
Cotton, some self-dyed.
Machine piecing, machine quilting.

I am fascinated by space, light, and movement. With these elements I try to express my feelings, thoughts, and reflections. *Space Travel* represents life as a segment in space and time. The color-tracks moving through space resemble the paths of human lives. Each color demands its part of space, influencing the others while not disturbing any other. The tracks move close to others yet stay separate. Each has a bright and dark side, each is once in the foreground, then in the background, each begins and ends outside the picture, in the indefinite.

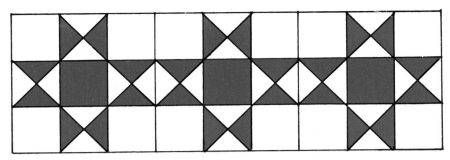

Blocks set solid.

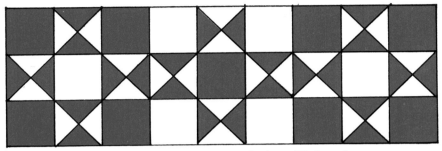

Pattern becomes a form of Shoofly when dark and light colors are alternated from block to block.

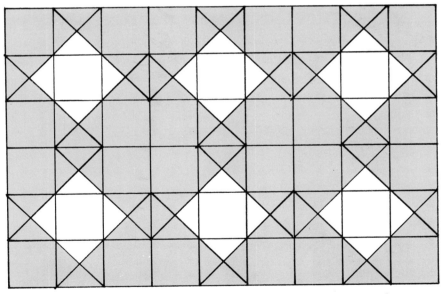

Ohio Star pattern—the color sequence has been changed so that a whole new pattern emerges.

Windblown Square

Set with alternate plain blocks, the design creates an entirely different quilt than when set solid.

FARBGEWITTER (COLOR STORM)
59" x 65"
Cotton, silk, chintz, mixed fabric, hand-dyed and hand-painted fabric.
Machine piecing, hand quilting.

This quilt, featuring a block of an unusual shape, is part of a series which I made using an original crazy-piecing technique. I worked for a time with a kite-shaped block, but then changed to a block with four different sides which tessellated in *Color Storm*. I want the viewer to have to search for the actual block. When I work in series I can see the many possibilities in one design and then develop them.

80

LATTICE WORKS II
67½" x 55"
Cotton, hand-dyed cotton, metallic thread.
Machine piecing, machine quilting.

After selecting this simple quilt block and playing with the design on paper, I discovered the different effects that resulted from varying the direction and placement of the blocks. After choosing a few promising combinations, I tested colors on paper.

I experimented with three main design areas: the foreground lattice, the background lattice, and the background. Each area was assigned a separate color scheme. Before starting construction I worked out all the general color ideas on paper, making final selections of actual fabrics as I went along. The interaction of the colors was fascinating, particularly as they fell against the background of changing gray values. I plan to continue this series.

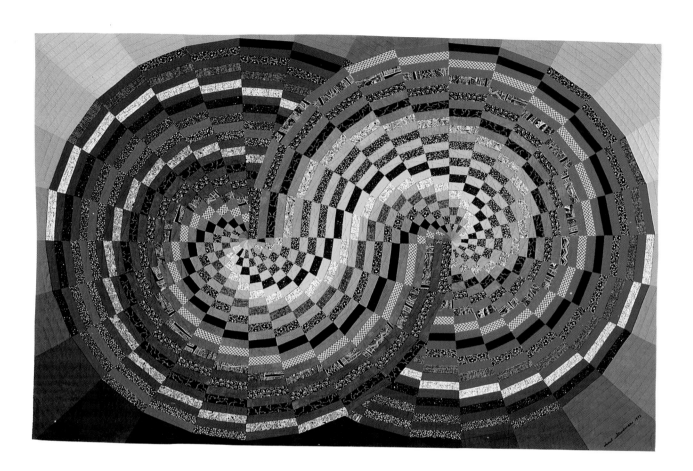

WHEELS OF COLOR
49″ x 73″
Commercial cotton, hand-dyed cotton.
Machine piecing, hand appliqué, hand quilting, machine quilting.

W*heels of Color* is the eighth in my series of spiral/circular quilts using a 15°
wedge shape. In 1991, when I moved to Whidbey Island, Washington, from
Houston, Texas, I took some of Nina and Eric Morti's hand-dyed fabrics with me.
Their red to yellow to blue fabrics inspired this quilt that I sketched as we drove
cross-country. As the design evolved I found I needed to dye even more fabrics to
complete the color wheel. The wheels symbolize the full circle my life has taken as
I return to my birthplace, the Pacific Northwest.

SKY/WIND VARIATIONS 2
51″ x 86½″
Cotton, silk taffeta.
Machine piecing, machine quilting.

On the surface, this quilt refers to air, wind, movement, and literal space. Below the surface, the quilt is about time: the passage of time in the making of the quilt itself, as well as in the maker's life, and the notion of "water under the bridge." Our lives are made up of pieces of experience, and my quilts are metaphors for that collective experience that is a life. We all seem to be seeking some sense of order, some pattern and rhythm in our lives. A pieced quilt may be the closest some of us come to that kind of order.

CHANGING PLANES
74″ x 72″
Cotton, cotton/linen blend; cotton batting.
Strip piecing, machine appliqué, machine quilting.

I started making quilts nearly 20 years ago. For the past 10 years I've explored the creation of visual planes or layers, one in front of another. I've also been investigating the effects of value gradations. Because I had no depth perception in my early years, I have been intrigued by the way value gradations can create a three-dimensional effect. I like the way a color adjacent to the light end of the gradation looks different from that same color next to the dark end. To emphasize the pun inherent in my title, I've put fabric with an airplane print on the back of the quilt.

84

TOBE (TO FLY)
72½" x 76"
Cotton.
Hand piecing, machine piecing, hand quilting.

Year after year, environmental pollution kills many species of animals and plants. The number of butterflies that fly in to visit our garden has diminished over the last few years. I appeal to the world to remember our responsibility to save nature for our next generation! The inspiration for my quilt came from an 18th-century European wallpaper design.

SPONSORS

♦

We received significant help from two corporate sponsors in producing this book. We are very grateful for their financial assistance and their continuing interest in providing fine fabrics to quiltmakers.

P&B Textiles

Creators of 100% cotton prints and solids that inspire and fulfill the needs of quiltmakers worldwide

and

South Sea Imports

Manufacturer of many fine quilting fabrics and sole producer of the Mary Ellen Hopkins fabric collection.

INDEX

TRAVELING EXHIBIT SCHEDULE

◆

Thirty quilts from Visions—The Art of the Quilt will travel to three venues during
1993.

Omnigrid ®
Creating a Revolution in Rotary Cutting

A generous grant from Omnigrid has helped to make the traveling exhibit possible.
We are grateful for their support.

Colorado Springs Pioneers Museum, Colorado Springs, Colorado
January 23, 1993–March 28, 1993

Museum of the American Quilter's Society, Paducah, Kentucky
April 17, 1993–August 28, 1993

William A. Farnsworth Library and Art Museum, Rockland, Maine
October 31, 1993–January 3, 1994

◆

For information regarding membership in Quilt San Diego, write to
Quilt San Diego
9747 Business Park Avenue, #228, San Diego, CA 92131

◆

Other Fine Quilting Books From C & T Publishing

Appliqué 12 Easy Ways!, Elly Sienkiewicz
Baltimore Beauties and Beyond (2 volumes), Elly Sienkiewicz
Crazy Quilt Handbook, Judith Montano
Heirloom Machine Quilting, Harriet Hargrave
Imagery on Fabric, Jean Ray Laury
Isometric Perspective, Katie Pasquini-Masopust
Landscapes & Illusions, Joen Wolfrom
The Magical Effects of Color, Joen Wolfrom
Mastering Machine Appliqué, Harriet Hargrave
Story Quilts, Mary Mashuta
Visions—Quilts of a New Decade, Quilt San Diego
3 Dimensional Design, Katie Pasquini

For more information write for a free catalog from
C & T Publishing
P.O. Box 1456
Lafayette, CA 94549
(1-800-284-1114)